El libro

detesto leer

The

I Hate to Read

Book

Jimmy Huston

Dedicado a Sarah de 11 años, Sean de 13 años, y Mark de 60 años, quienes detestan leer.

Mis más sinceras disculpas a la Sra. Pickett.

Dedicated to Sarah 11, Sean 13, and Mark 60, who all hate to read.

With all due apologies to Mrs. Pickett.

Capítulo uno

No continúes a la siguiente página.

Encontrarás palabras en ella.

Chapter One

Do not turn the page.

There are words there.

Intenté advertirte.

Ahora encontrarás más.

Encontrarás letras, palabras, y enunciados.

Incluso párrafos.

Pero nada más.

Bueno, y también páginas.

Detesto leer. Detesto leerlas todas.

I tried to warn you.

Now there will be even more.

There will be letters, and words, and sentences.

Even paragraphs.

But nothing bigger.

Okay, pages.

I hate to read. I hate to read them all.

Pero bien, si ya llegaste hasta aquí, hay que acabar pronto.

Continúa a la siguiente página.

But as long as you've gotten this far, let's get this over with.

Turn the page.

Capítulo 2

Los capítulos hacen que parezca que lees más pronto, pero no es suficiente.

Los capítulos siempre comienzan en la página derecha, dejando la de la izquierda en blanco.

Así se acaba más pronto el libro.

No me importa.

Detesto leer.

Chapter 2

Chapters make reading seem to go fast – but not fast enough.

Chapters always start on the right-side page, so the left page can be blank.

Then it goes even faster.

I don't care.

I hate to read.

Capítulo 3

Ves? Se está acabando pronto, pero aun así...

Detesto leer.

Chapter 3

See. It's going pretty fast, but even so...

I hate to read.

No me gustan las palabras grandes.

I don't like big words.

No me gustan
las palabras
pequeñas.

I don't like
little
words.

Si hay muchas palabras, detesto leerlas. Si hay muchas palabras, detesto leerlas.

If there are a lot of words, I hate to read. If there are a lot of words, I hate to read.

O si no hay.

De todas maneras, detesto leer.

Or not.

Still, I hate to read.

No intenten engañarme con dibujos.

Detesto leer.

Don't try to fool me with pictures.

I hate to read.

No intenten complacerme con buenas historias.

Héroes y villanos.

Historias románticas.

Salvar al mundo.

Finales felices.

Protagonistas (Ni siquiera busques esta palabra).

Déjenme en paz.

Detesto leer.

Don't try to please me with good stories.

Heroes and villains.

Boy meets girl.

Save the day.

Happy endings.

Protagonists. (Don't even look it up.)

Give me a break.

I hate to read.

Aunque sea divertido, detesto leer.

Y usualmente, no lo es.

Popó.

Bueno, eso sí fue divertido.

Pero aún así, detesto leer.

Even if it's funny, I hate to read.

And it's usually not.

Poop.

Now that's funny.

But I still hate to read.

Ni siquiera quiero hablar de poesía.

    Porque la escriben en rima.

    Peor que mi prima.

¿Lo ves? ¿A quién le importa?

A mí no.

Detesto leer.

Don't even get me started on poetry.

    They make it rhyme.

    Most of the time.

See? Who cares?

Not me.

I hate to read.

No me importa si mi hermana ama leer.

No me importa si mi hermano ama leer.

No me importa quién ama la lectura.

No importa.

Yo detesto leer.

I don't care if my sister likes to read.

I don't care if my brother likes to read.

I don't care who likes to read.

It doesn't matter.

I hate to read.

Capítulo cinco

Aquí comienza otro capítulo.

Tómate un descanso.

Detesto leer.

Chapter Five

Here's another chapter.

Take a break.

I hate to read.

Por cierto, más vale que este libro no sea un truco para obligarme a leer.

Ya te lo dije, detesto leer.

No es un truco.

De verdad detesto leer.

By the way, do not let this book be a trick to get me to read.

I already told you. I hate to read.

It's not a trick.

I hate to read. Really.

Capítulo seis

¿Qué pasó con el Capítulo cuatro?

Calla y continúa. Ya casi termina.

¿Mencioné ya que detesto leer?

Chapter Six

What happened to Chapter Four?

Shut up and keep going. It's almost over.

Did I mention that I hate to read?

Capítulo siete

A veces palabras se desacomodan las.

Qué difícil leer vuelve.

Detesto leer.

Chapter Seven

Sometimes words the mixed up get.

That hard it makes.

I hate to read.

No me gustan los libros largos.

No me gustan los libros cortos.

No me gustan los diccionarios.

No me gustan las enciclopedias.

Detesto leer.

(Los libros de cómics no cuentan)

I don't like long books.

I don't like short books.

I don't like dictionaries.

I don't like encyclopedias.

I hate to read.

(Comic books don't count.)

No me gusta leer en voz alta.

No me gusta leer en silencio.

A veces finjo estar leyendo.

Ojalá este libro se acabe pronto.

Detesto leer.

I don't like reading out loud.

I don't like reading quietly.

Sometimes I pretend to be reading.

I wish this book was over.

I hate to read.

No me gustan los libros que intentan asustarme.

No me hagan llorar.

No intenten engañarme.

No me sorprendan.

No me dejen en suspenso.

No me enseñen nada.

Detesto leer.

I don't like books that try to scare me.

Don't make me cry.

Don't try to fool me.

Don't surprise me.

Don't leave me hanging.

Don't teach me stuff.

I hate to read.

No me gusta leer historias acerca de ponis.

No me gusta leer historias de piratas.

No me gusta leer historias sobre junglas, océanos, o el espacio.

Si hay que leer, ya las detesto.

Sobre todo no me gustan los reportes de lectura.

Detesto leer.

I don't like to read stories about ponies.

I don't like to read stories about pirates.

I don't like to read stories about jungles or oceans or outer space.

If I have to read it, I already hate it.

I especially don't like book reports.

I hate to read.

No me digas que leer es bueno para mí.

Que bañarse es bueno para mí.

Que los vegetales son buenos para mí.

Que la medicina es buena para mí.

No me importa.

Detesto leer.

Don't tell me reading is good for me.

Baths are good for me.

Vegetables are good for me.

Medicine is good for me.

I don't care.

I hate to read.

No me digas que leer es educativo.

Es un truco.

Cada año lo hacen más difícil.

Primer grado, segundo grado, tercer grado. Más y más difícil.

Déjenme en paz.

Detesto leer.

Don't tell me that reading is educational.

It's all a trick.

Every year they make it harder.

First grade, second grade, third grade. Harder and harder.

Leave me alone.

I hate to read.

Capítulo noventa y cinco

Incluso en la página 465, detesto leer.

Pero por más que deteste leer, siempre se siente bien…

Chapter Ninety-five

Even on page 465, I still hate to read.

But as much as I hate to read, it always feels good....

...terminar un libro.

FIN

...to finish a book.

THE END

Ya puedes dejar de leer.

Se acabó.

Estas solo son tonterías para la gente que no detesta leer, y de alguna manera terminaron en esta página.

Habrá más cosas que leer en *www.i-hate-to-read.com.*

Si quisieras escribirnos una reseña positiva en alguna parte, lo agradeceríamos mucho.

Si quieres escribirnos una reseña negativa, envíala a *heystupid@i-hate-to-read.com.*

Tenemos una colección de libros igual de ilustres y/o ridículos disponibles en *www.cosworthpublishing.com.*

Pero los detestarás.

You can stop reading now.

It's over.

This is just some gibberish for people who do *not* hate to read, and have somehow stumbled onto this page.

We will have more words available at *www.i-hate-to-read.com.*

If you'd like to write a nice review somewhere, it would be greatly appreciated.

If you'd like to write a nasty review, send it to *heystupid@i-hate-to-read.com.*

There is an excellent selection of equally distinguished and/or ridiculous books available at *www.cosworthpublishing.com.*

But you won't like them.

Nothing here.

Aquí ya no hay nada.

Still nothing.

Ni aquí.

What exactly are you looking for? Don't you realize you're reading unnecessarily?

¿Qué es lo que buscas? ¿No te has dado cuenta que estás leyendo sin razón?

Why?

¿Por qué?

Okay, maybe reading isn't always so awful. But, what I *REALLY* hate --

Bueno, tal vez leer no siempre es malo. Pero, lo que DE VERDAD detesto --

I hate to write. (Maybe you noticed.)

Detesto escribir (Tal vez ya lo notaste).

You're still reading?

¿Sigues leyendo?

Ya, deja este libro.

Bueno, si tu no pararás, yo sí. Vamos afuera a jugar.

Put the book down.

Okay, if you're not going to stop, I will. Let's go outside and play.

Other Books (that you will hate) by Jimmy Huston

Otros libros (que detestarás) por Jimmy Huston

...and I Hate Math 2

Nate-Nate the Christmas Snake

The Dyslexic Handbook: Genius Edition

Cussing for Kids!: Etiquette for the Profane

The Attention Deficit Disorder Hyperactive Cookbook: Puzzle Edition

Autism for Beginners: Surfing the Spectrum

The OCD Funbook: Really?

The Bedtime Book of Bad Dreams: Dozing Dangerously

Baby's First Instruction Manual: How To Be the Center of the Universe

Rat BLEEP and Alien Poop: Not for Parents at All

The Big Beautiful Book of Burping, Belching, and Barfing

The Book Book: Inside the Inside Story

Why Can't Mommy Spend More Time with Me?

How to Write This Book: You're Going To Be the Author

The Amazing, Stupendous, Extraordinary, and Somewhat Unusual SPINNING BOOK

That Damn Little Angel

The Snake Test: True? False? Maybe?

Is This Your First Funeral?: A Child's Primer

The First Apology Is the Worst

It's Not Easy Being Mister Ladybug

Don't Go to College, Go to Europe for Less

Dead Is the New Sick: An Insider's Guide to Senility, Paranoia, and Curmudgery

www.byjimmyhuston.com
www.cosworthpublishing.com

www.ingramcontent.com/pod-product-compliance
Lightning Source LLC
Chambersburg PA
CBHW041524120626
46551CB00018B/2561